PAX AMERICANA

Also by Paul Otremba

The Currency

Pax Americana

Paul Otremba

Four Way Books
Tribeca

For Holly

Please direct all inquiries to:
Editorial Office
Four Way Books
POB 535, Village Station
New York, NY 10014
www.fourwaybooks.com

Library of Congress Cataloging-in-Publication Data

Otremba, Paul.
[Poems. Selections]
Pax Americana / Paul Otremba.
pages ; cm
ISBN 978-1-935536-56-7 (acid-free paper)
I. Title.
PS3615.T74A6 2015
811'.6--dc23
2014030217

This book is manufactured in the United States of America and printed on acid-free paper.

Four Way Books is a not-for-profit literary press. We are grateful for the assistance we receive from individual donors, public arts agencies, and private foundations.

This publication is made possible with public funds from the New York State Council on the Arts, a state agency.

State of the Arts
NYSCA

[clmp]

We are a proud member of the Council of Literary Magazines and Presses.
Distributed by University Press of New England
One Court Street, Lebanon, NH 03766

Contents

"Deserve's got nothing to do with it." —Will Munny

Auspices

I want to think of them as having been
sent up ahead, the swift ones bearing news
of tides to follow, so we might get ready,
the dark swells and dips of starlings—or grackles—

being that impressive to watch in winter
gather nightly above the downtown square,
these grackles—or starlings—mostly unnoticed
until their purpose tips to overwhelming,

where surely some word has been given us.
Mostly I find them unpleasant, a grimy
congress of incomprehensibles bathing
in oil-stained puddles slowly cooking off

parking lots, or at trash cans, their sharp heads
stabbing after this soggy morsel of bun,
now this corruption of meat. Mostly they are
a nuisance. A tree unwise to walk nearby;

a beam risky to leave your car beneath.
And on the Internet—where my haphazard
compulsive search for understanding leads me—
someone's posted a poorly captured and cut

video of "a starling (or a grackle,
sorry)," he or she writes, who's just started
digging into another bird on the lawn,
while a bored looking rabbit and we look on

this meal. The eating continued for hours,
we're told, and the music the maker's spliced in
portends that this "appetite is tremendous,"
warns, "keep your eye on the barrel, a sparrow."

Pax Americana

I began reading. It was like enlightenment,
what someone once described as an act of remembrance,
like here in the book with the many colored plates,
the one with the skeleton demonstrating the horse
as its memento of solidness, like pocketing a few stones
while visiting the ruins, these dice to cast later as fortunes,
or the memory of a museum with that odd print of a skeleton
posed before a rhinoceros and a stand of broken columns,
which meant to say something about perspective or mutability,
but equally the crowding over of a scarcity of resources—
I thought of the Barbarians entering the Eternal City,
and I was in their ranks.

(In the reality
where we enter the city as triumphant conquerors,
we're asked to dinner parties, given household gods
as affectionate tokens. Against our forces, the affection
and corked wine aim their insurgency. We receive
announcements not to pull over, to avoid the market.
Some remember a promise. Some say it is difficult to make a life here.)

If only I could see into the gaze, and therefore have a word
to translate that space between bone and column, bone
and armored skin. And in this way the atmosphere affects me,
the occupation finds its shape, an archway from inside to inside.
Whether you're guilty yourself, Roman, is not the question.

To the Architects of Our Present Misfortune

Do you know that movie where people fall
asleep each night only to have the world
redrawn, their roles recast, each day's newness
the result of alien technology
and a shifty, collaborating doctor?

A person would feel bad. You see the hero
rise up, but you know you're not him, at least
the probability you prize so much
tells us so. Or how in Italy once
a man tried dreaming a place fit for you,

and what he thought of was ice and the rank
sad mouths he set you in. It helps to acquire
an image, to gather things you can hold
in hand to grease the bouncer, then to stake
your bet at the table, take the house to the bank.

It helps to imagine the air accruing
not much else beyond desperation when passed
from lungs to lungs as in a parlor game.
The kids may still know what that means even
without having a word for it, without having

seen one. We'll have to owe you for the tips
about the pleas and shells, how to divide
a piece of paper infinitely, how
the name of the person whose extension
we are calling will always be Legion.

About certain things it's best not to feign
ambivalence: your arm in a vice; fire
tracking ash across what were once tract homes
in suburban California. But meeting
a wolf you think you might just understand

the mechanism of a jaw, the sole
purpose of teeth, how lonely it can get
out there. We were not really built for this.
We invested a canary in the shaft,
and all we got back was a thin flute's thin song.

The snake was only ever meant to learn
what happened to the bird; the cat, the snake;
the coyote, the tangible evidence
of our growing despondency. Fellow members,
I know it's our blind faith in speculation

that keeps the meat from rot, that lights the rooms
we need to cross to reach still other rooms
for love and thoughts, artistic machinations.
If only that cock Crassus had shown up,
the boardroom would have fallen before me.

Epistle

If I thought it would help, B______, I'd offer gossip's juicy flash
Of thigh, tales of So-&-So's drunken fumbles, or an update
From the capital, where every day we suffer exiles
Of more friends. Here's evidence of the small insurrections
That keep me in this mood: I wrote, "It's the creature we are;
When the animal / is sick, it lies down.
Not difficult, then, / to reach our first moral lesson."
I read and I wrote, "*whenever it is a damp, drizzly November*
In my soul, / the animal would lie down if I'd let it."
Which provides alibi or comfort, like an anecdote or joke:
A man sits in a bar at a table crowded with empties;
And when he adjusts his arm beneath his head (bottles knocking
Against each other, bottles sent to the floor), in the shattering,
His voice announces to no one and everyone, "I'll pay for it,
I'll pay for everything;" and we get the immense
Sadness of it. There's a punch line so we can smile.
The story helps. Like living next to water helps.
"The way to be happy and stay so," a poet's letter starts,
And I want to stop reading. The stomach is another thing.
I'd recommend *lechón asado*, fried plantains, and a pint of good beer.
I'd recommend braised lamb shank steeped with rosemary and olives,
Ripe grapes crushed on the tongue. I like the task of it, the clear arc
From conception to accomplishment—the pans drying at the sink.
You might say "meditation." There's the blade's smooth rhythm
And a fragrance expelled from the small, stiff leaves.
You might say "immersion." Dreams are another thing.
One minute I'm kissing a mouth I once knew, and as I open

Against it, her mouth is full of water; the next, they hover above me:
My instructors, my captors. Their looks tell me
To sit, pay attention. Their looks tell me there are consequences.
I want to believe in the moral, and if not the moral, then the story,
A structure not resembling the chemistry set spills and combustions
You claim for these events. But if not the story, then the reading of it,
The insistence on a shape, "a function that is wholly realistic,
And continually born anew." It's not despite life's meanings
Happiness is found here. Just the other night on television
When the heroes arrived at the goal of their quest
For friendship and love and discovered instead of redemption
A hole rent through the earth, the vampire with a soul
(That's the other one) resigned: "Feels like we ought to have known."

Clarissa in Uptown

Like a great big clock, you wouldn't look for it
if you didn't already know it was there, I mean,
a person doesn't just wake up one morning
thinking, *I will buy the flowers myself,* someone's
got to put the flowers in there in the first place,
the idea of flowers, that there should be such
arrangements and a will to walk it through
from seed to hothouse to truck to cellophane,
a person doesn't do that, well, you might,
perhaps *you'd* think of it spontaneously
like a preference for sour over sweet, the tongue
knows, we say, or it's the nose that has a mind
for such things—you draw the tip
of the pen to your tongue and say,
I'll buy the flowers myself, and it should have something
of the world in it, cars and a city, fashionable
Korean taco trucks and organic cocktail bars,
a whole way of life expressed by the way
you hold a fork, by having the choice there
fanned out across the table before you,
the big fork, little fork, and knife, a choice
you made before the menus were lifted
so the bread could arrive, a way of life you extract
from chewed up fingers furtively clearing your plate,
the biggest gulp and all the sugary sips you can glean,
you try to make something with a little dignity.

As Hero

And from the flight deck the announcement came.
And we could all return to work the next day

secure in our collective sense of mission or relief.
A series of underground caves, or channels,

I thought, our country as a porousness, shooting pool
in the bar as a tacit belief. We were in the capital then,

where the concrete barriers made to look
like flowerpots were all understood as flowerpots.

When we talk, I'd like to address your more original,
your more spontaneous decision. A cable mini-series

is how I saw it last night. In the parable, the student
asks the teacher whether resisting the fascists

or staying home to help his sick mother is right.
Of course, no one actually wills an extended stay,

we said, and in that we'd found our lesson.
Years of this across the daily feed and still hard

to connect what the mind reads with sustenance.
You either get to be the kind of person who resists

what's coming or who helps dig under. Make it happen.
But if we must be more tractable, a coarse netting will do.

Cicero on the Death of His Child

Dear B_____, when a limb's bruised
and swollen, we say
the animal is sick.
Likewise the heart. A brute

knows this; so how much easier do you think
for the wise? Experience
reveals such things.

Returning to the house, M_____ observed
there's a space
near the back of a cat's neck,

where if you make a cut
deep enough, it will become so
unaccountably enraged, you'd understand

what the poet meant singing
of Achilles. I found myself thinking
about a room—

my first impression of being
inside a room—not like a fresco freshly painted,
but a bit of arm or shield

on a shard of pottery
among the walls of the fallen city. In that room,
a broken vase, a cat running,
and my mother's anger.

Fear and Trembling

I learned to trust in mechanisms. The switch
flipped for illumination. If the same lamp
at night were found beside the bed when waking,
hit every third step on descent into the room:

they'd be there. Hit every step: the room
was there. If the ball—heard—knocked the vase,
the cat went running. If the ball thrown—but
unheard, unseen—stopped, and the vase fell

anyway, the cat went running. Both ended
equally in their anger. For months days
would end/begin. I turned

the lamp on/off in odd numbers, in evens.
The results each morning remained
indeterminate: I still woke here.

***

And waking from the dream, I knew the ship would come,
arriving from the island in three days' time; then

to fertile Phthia I'll go, and not before,
because this is your sentence, what you've made of me,

because I could not convince you, could not undo
the politician's fear, the poet's shadow play,

the artisan's insecurities, or the honeyed
argument, words as substanceless as cakes in the mouth

of the mind; I will go, and spare the guards the slight
embarrassment of money; I will go, and my friends

will still be hated; go because you ask, lawgiver,
for whom it is given to bring the greatest good,

the greatest harm, for you will leave nothing to chance
when you perform as jury and executioner.

***

And one hand feels the heart beneath the fingers,
while the other hand closes around the knife.
And to arrive at this height, I'm required
to follow but not follow you. For if

I wait to know one billiard ball striking
another, I will never get here; and if
I wait to confirm that every creature strives
to fulfill a longing, some endgame for life

implicit in its opening, a mold
suffused, I will never get here; and if
I claim, therefore, "the philosopher's mortal,"
each time I utter it (so more than belief),

I still could not arrive at the knife, or the wind
on the hill like the breath that pleads against the hand.

***

In the Rembrandt when your messenger arrives
the boy cannot see, and so perhaps when asked later,

the boy says, "Yes," when he's thinking only of the wind,
but it helps him to say it, to repeat "the ram," "the thicket,"

until they become the inextricable elements of a chain
of how the day began one way and ended where it did,

how *the sun shone / As it had to*, and tomorrow would again,
which he'd wager on more than the voice

he only now occasionally addresses (now only in his head),
and sometimes when he senses the slow tightening of sleep

the boy imagines some point off in the sky, then himself
as seen from it, then another, and still others beyond it,

until all he feels is a vastness, a terror he'd heard sung
in the old songs about thefts crossroads treasons murders.

***

Coda: Theory of the Maggot

The problem is that there should even be a sensation
          of being held by your body,

that you could feel *in* this while not *of* it; therefore, *here*
          and *where-the-world-begins*;

or rather, *not-here* and—
                                        Which is the grieving composer's
          misguided point, the soprano singing

over and over *lacrimosa, lacrimosa* until you can forget
          your own name; which is why

in the story when George Clinton asks, "play like your Momma
          just died," Eddie Hazel does.

The Hive

"To the Age its Art, to Art its Freedom"

New techniques, material
layers, so a body
of work glued together—we found

that break showing honey.
Oh, Vienna, you cannot move!
But always in the same period-dress

gardens and words
feel stepped-on.
Their progressions curdle

behind our profiles
like eggs, or an obvious Typhon
if only you know the handshakes

for entrance to the dance.
And Mal? Your strings
still echo full of wolves.

At the end of the day
they call us where?
Just some hope a cue summons

within you. Here, I submit
a list of my complaints.
I did but taste the field.

Communiqué

So a speck crosses your eye, so
the oily smack of wings?
The you you talk to in there?
The huddled masses
over the rat-road? Don't worry,
we can now live chat
from the summit, and whatever
we can't divide in nicely
we'll carry back with us: the oxygen
tank's husk, a soreness webbing
from our shortened breath,
the site of that. The flag is up,
so come out with a show
of hands. No funny business.
Just this once we'll shake it
off and move forward. You can trust
I'll catch the explosive
core before it hits the floor.
We've trained for this. This once
we'll look for where we'll find
the thing the edict says
we're not to touch.
Closer, come closer, as you would
speak to your pet. You see,
there is this circumference,
an edge against what feels like
voices ringing in the dome's bell.

Just this once,
    the can at your ear may
produce a bloom.

Dioscuri

Two animals, like horses, running, two
horses running

side by side, what we're up against,
the trough's translucency, open to the sun—

I am bound to look up at you,
my Bonnie, my ocean.

Where was it we first heard of
the egg, the part unshelling the whole,

the whole stocked with gold provisions,
this immanent suspicion

you're on the wrong side?
It requires a move, a stacking

of one teetering acrobat over his brother
before your whole being can retreat,

clicking off stones with a traveler's cane—
a suspicion you're on the right side

sinks and edifies.
What will you do down there?

And of those flecks we once called sparks
off the anvil, those stars,

our folksy wisdom about their light
and where the light went?

El Hombre

They build such elaborate
machines to have
the cage drop,
the marble rise.
Down the slide, haecceity
made its sudden leap.
What we need is a yes-man,
a purer obfuscation,
the right-now-of-it
alert like fur.
Knowing the individual strands
from the forest
and the agents of our sentences,
to get a full stomach and
a stained mouth.
Some claim it came as a voice,
a large booming gasbag
himself deciding, You, go
over there and feel bad about it;
you, sit near me.
Many have written
songs on that theme,
some you can even march to
or perform for a balancing act.
I feel like I remember it,
that it is there
to be found, your own tail

you might discover in your own
mouth when stumbling
over it. In a different time
we might have said a ring makes
its depression in wax, this here,
this bowl of it the air holds,
between the faces kissing and not
the candlestick. What
sprang from this terrible rock.

The Apparition

Like the electron cloud in its cloudy diagram,
now you see it, now the heat-

flash on your skin from rope burn,
dog-eared page, heel

and spike—you can call it back,
a wall, perhaps, to drum

to prove permeable. They used to say the soul
gets in like that,

and so we had meat to knock against,
a tin plate for ringing out the bars.

The without-which-nothing-so-
you-hunger came next,

or like my fists held out—Pick one.
If the animal were kinder, you'd think

they'd make that the standard,
remove the pressure from

the throat as delicate as a paper nest.
On this condition: what you have in hive

we hear first, a humming, an approach.
It is without any support, really,

your words, this container full
of communal beetles,

a vacancy you're committed to. Here, then,
the insect's carapace.

From the Provinces

i. The Argument

—St. Paul, Minnesota, Winter 1998

Everyday the bubble's growing, and we feel
the new money as it rivers through the city,
depositing jobs, apartments, the revitalized
geography. Growing up here, we know

the myth surrounding the corner of Selby/Dale,
where kids like us could shoulder-tap for beer
and hail sex from the walls. By the time I moved in
all that remained of the mystery was an attitude.

Even here we have art, a few cafés, ethnic
and upscale fusion cuisines, garden patios
(but all east of the corner, where the street makes
for the cathedral, the old families). The old

money of Victorian houses is erased by snow,
a white line expanding on my windowsill.

ii. The Summit

—University of Minnesota Arboretum, Fall 1998

We meet outside the city to discuss the mind
of poetry, and crowning the speaker's head,
the arboretum fills up the conference room's
window: an epiphany of maples and the papery
consciousness of birch against the sky's blue
concentration flag the roots of our connections.
But reading the daily papers—from New York,
London—was a form of recognition (but east
of the corner) that events would continue,
so the end of history was beginning to look
a lot like history. Stopping along the trail,
a single ornamental maple becomes the sole
object of attention. Around the maple, the day
is calm and clear. There's an intimacy to this.

iii. Stray Cat

—Fall 1998

History's in the houses built along this street
In the café's back room, there are three of us

behind the cathedral, on the hill above the city
me reading alone, so I hear their conversation

the historical, meaning not those who live here
One woman, a Croat, talks about a friend still

or have lived here—their families—for over
over "there," what she heard, a young woman

a century. We buy up the historical to make
pregnant, and some men came—as always—

room for young professionals (white, European)
and afterwards the town found all three dead:

for restaurants, shops, and condominiums
child, mother, and what was placed in her womb

iv. The Menu

—*Winter 1998*

Plates of salmon, gravlax, cold-
smoked, hot-smoked, blinis, steamed
mussels, fennel bulb braised in Pernod,
carpaccio, extra virgin olive oil, (Even
at the edge of the capital…), prosciutto
wrapped melon, soup of the day, white
chocolate-cayenne-spiced-tenderloin
with lobster foam and white bean cassoulet,
(…we are inside the capital), slivers
of truffles, fresh catch flown in that morning,
blackberry, blackberry-veal stock reduction,
winter vegetable risotto, cheeses, fresh
honeycomb, figs, desserts made daily,
wine cellar available for private parties.

v. Divination

—September 26, 1998

The heart is weighty, you will prosper. *Our hands*
had to remain behind our heads. This came out

tightly coiled, but no bruise, you will prosper.
We were first gathered in the field. In the stomach,

clumps of grass (*They brought us to the garden),*
whole apple seeds with the poison still intact.

Faces touching the ground. This remains hidden.
I turned once to ask if there was an inspector.

A rich, liquid-like gold. *A policeman replied,*
"I am the inspector." The smell inside the horse

is of a strong oil burning. *One man shot us, but others*
were around in the garden. Keep these ashes

fashioned to your skin, they can protect you.
I survived because I remained totally dead.

vi. The Election

—November 3, 1998

Even here we have our skirmishes. We ask for
a politician who is not a politician, *the ancient*
myths of public Suffering and Humiliation:
the cross and the pillory. The forearm smash.

We ask for the river to carve out revitalization,
the spectacle of suffering, of methodically
establishing the conditions of suffering.
The public asks for an art to reflect the public,

not because it regrets the absence of real
suffering. (An arm-lock, a twisted leg.)
We ask for the impeachment of indiscretion,
the pure gesture which separates Good from Evil.

Even here we get the results as they happen.
The spectator does not wish for actual suffering.

vii. Envoi

We wander out in circles—
thick swarm'd—imagining a room

rising out of this one, history's
Muzak looped in the speakers,

riding the continuous fattening
of the bubble. We divine

our profits and collect now.
We throw out the net. Dredge

the wealth of distances. We cast
our vote-of-no-confidence over

the vast regions of the provinces.
Demand the impeachment

of power as payment for our own.
We accumulate the ethereal hive.

Ecology

When the hive won't come back again, call it
an unfortunate precedent. When stares blink

on-off, star-like, it's the confession's reticence,
a smudged flock from Grand Isle. So we can know

the yield from fallow, say you'll come for us.
If before rising waters, then the core steeps

through the flesh, lights up the jaw. So the waves
return your alarm but older, birds work against

discarded drums. In their songs, ice-melt
come suddenly. In the red of that picture,

the nickeled stream, say I turned away but had to
carry it. When the face in mirror, call it irises pooled

in phosphorus. So we will know how to find our way
out again, call it industrious. When the sidewalks

appeared sludged with cherry-blossoms,
they said heat swelled the eyes open too early.

Of Them That Sold Doves

It begins with labor, what keeps this machine
in sync within the larger gears and coils,
the 1s and 0s chattering across channels

of labyrinthine wires, and those tumblers
on what appear to be perfectly shaped lawns
sheened like lakes under gasoline. Or try

this stick and rock and a powerful need
to move a bigger rock, you've got leverage.
But the machines come later, so this leaf

afloat in a river—something keeps it up,
a kind of tension, say, the leaf wanting
not to fall through but not contributing much else

in defense of that. The water, well,
it's just water; it doesn't really have a choice;
I mean, it was there, and labor works

like that, holding back its own flood, except
when it breaks, leaves like money running
everywhere, except back into the water.

In an Adirondack with You

Well, there's the one about the boy who fell
off the swing. Because the wind picked up.
Because after three days, I've gone outside
into the heat and heard you laugh across
long distances, crossing the road that cuts
the little cake-village, the field in view,
and behind that the spine of pine trees curved
in the sun. It's the only joke I remember.
How are the rains this year? Has the fox returned?
I don't believe in a redemptive nature,
I'm not sure I ever have. But you see,
I grew crooked in the great Midwestern
suburb pent, bending to a music of doorbells
knocked off their hinges and the greasy burn
of gasoline balloons with newspaper wicks,
while the games kept on after the lamppost
blinked in the cul-de-sac. I've been to Idaho.
I've stood at Shelley's feet but only thought
of fat rendered in the sand. I couldn't recall
a single line of Corso. I have tried to live
with compassion. So here, a list of people—
where if I could go back, were permitted
a run-in at the grocery store—whom I'd hug:
Hugo, Neil Diamond, Lowell the polar bear
but not of the letters. Still, the accidents
continue. In the shower of break-away glass,
I, too, may or may not have been drunk,

may or may not have fled the scene.
I have tried hard to live without regrets.
By now you will have traversed the field,
the brook, the smallest bone in your body,
the yellow gravel parking lot with yellow
dust on your shoes. I would not leave you
to explain things to the cops and multiple trips
to the plastic surgeon. I like your nose,
and when I need to, can conjure a face
around it, though obscured by smoke, giving
a little something for Henry and poor Paul,
before watching the lit tips dissolve
in the nothing that waits below the bridge.
I'm not sure I know how to praise anything
except food. Your pesto was delicious.
Perfect as the simple sandwich of pecorino
and soprosata near the *Piramide Cestia.*
Rivaling the generosity of peaches I ate
from a brown paper sack off a highway
in Texas. Have you ever danced a two-step?
Witnessed a XXX megaplex or a closed-circuit
execution? Is not stopping for hitchhikers
along certain stretches, under any circumstance,
as morally suspect as a bower? The theater
swells with the attentive crowd, and I am
not there, ting'd with mischief, leaving
a seat open for the stranger who usurps

the performance by setting fire to a trashcan.
I wouldn't hug Berryman. I'd hug Coleridge
of "Frost at Midnight," but only to line 48.
What I heard you say over the phone
through the noisy bar was "you are mist,"
which is what you said. Henceforth, all
condensation will be reviewed as felicitous.
How awkwardly we teeter on laps in this chair,
trying to nestle like a babushka doll.
I've never been to Moscow, but I've read
it's a place to grow sad in. The best
Hungarian food I've ever had was in Krakow.
The best Mexican food, Minneapolis.
Have you heard the one about the Russian
medical student who left his first class
because he'd be studying the pancreas, not life?
I hear the bell and follow you to the table.
Where I tell you about the Polish waitress
who, holding my credit card, asked, "And who
is Mr. Oatmeal?" Everyday I seem to break
for more dogs. Because nostalgia like longing
eats its own tail. Because it has no arms.

Epistle

Because sleep won't come well these days, these nights,
B_______, which are not new, which are a mind's spiraling
Off kilter—"were it not that I have bad dreams." And not the terror
You'd expect. Not the zombie horde or the shopping mall's collapse
But a trip to the observation deck, where your eye becomes
The bubble of glass you're looking through and beyond, a fish-eyed
Bulging toward that vault of black space punched lightly
With stars, "salt on an axe-blade." It stays with you,
The dull ache, the vague, bruising pressure. Not profound
Revelations, and I'm only indicted further
When on the mob show the sullen and unpromising son
Finds only a pointlessness—a nameless dread hung
From birth to death—to which the aging matriarch responds:
"What makes you think you're so special?" Still, I return there,
For if the clot breaks loose, bursting a pinhole leak,
"For if the sinewy thread my brain lets fall,"
For in my mind it arrives more often as the reproach
Of a Brooklyn mother: "What's it to you the universe is expanding?"
Which isn't exactly what she says in the movie
But how I've come to live with it. How I'm able to sleep it off
And wake up feeling strange—yet comfortable—
To be in bed. There's a meeting, a class, but the trail
Of stones isn't as pale as I'd thought in the sunlight.
It's just another way to keep a connection, to spend
My afternoon searching the etymology of "chunking the deuce"
And the music I heard on the spy show, which wasn't Barber's
"Adagio for Strings," but sad nonetheless, like we'd expect

Of things made to contain our "Prime Objects."
Keats intended something different, writing to Haydon
About "a Refuge as well as a Passion" against the sickness
Of money, bearing his likeness of Shakespeare to Margate.
Who thinks about fame anymore? Who wouldn't want
To infiltrate the warehouse, be cuffed to a chair and escape
With a paperclip, a dislocated shoulder, by seducing the guards,
If it meant the luxury of clear objectives while still having protocols
To break? To say over the encroaching steps and tension
Of violins, "I won't leave you," even though
You're wounded and we've been compromised?

Negative Theology

You were not dressed as a policeman,
or a fair amount of cured meats,
as a tomcat or mouser, the (*informal*) kitty,
the (*archaic*) grimalkin.

The gray roads here slope steeply.
There will be clouds above the state,
the aggregate of ice-flecks and mood stones
travelling at the height of speed.

When the time is not unripe,
come down, and boil down to
the sap with its attendant trace
of syrup on fingers lording over the page.

I didn't grow un-hungry in the cloister,
the room they had me enter
to make hollows in, to wrestle with
the point at which I can predict the story's

antagonists, find the vessel's keel.
Just a consideration of the facts.
Well, if that's what you want, it follows that
I should be permitted a sliding payment scale:

I offer this blasted hill and a lung spot,
a significant signature towards the ceasefire,
a spitting distance to the river,
the *amuse-bouche* or complimentary drink,

a brittle insight. You are neither
permeable, nor translucent, nor nebulous.
You are not octopus-armed
or armies there of. But neither are you

the rain's runoff harvested,
the warp and woof, the tincture drained,
the contents of this case made
typically of plastic or earthenware.

The Pure Products

Citizens, in the middle of America
I found myself as in a dark mood,
your emissaries arriving as sun
on chrome, as crosshairs marking shades
on a billboard, a shadowy threat
to take back an abstraction
gone abstractly missing. Because
the lesson is always descent,
we must enter at the end of hope
"until stript"—(sic)—"enough
for the sprout to thrive."
And from your shore,
the river appears full.
Let's say you are the hive
of sad ones who didn't know better.
The set of all things the eye sees
that includes the eye itself
is one way to found a morality;
a boot to the face before
a boot to the face is another.
In this river of fire it's best
to play the frog.
Then they hand you—they
who wish to God—
this floating device fashioned
from electrocution or this
version made of crude sludge,
but I'd rather have the trident, please,
the cat-o'-nine-tails, that measures out
to around six bucks if you lay
the dollar bills down end to end.

O America, to discover what
you've asked of me must I
climb through your tangled hair
after emerging from your mouth?
There is a place up ahead,
full of beaches and buffalo.
Put your ear to this bleached socket;
you can hear what we'll do
when we get there.

The Swiss Are Coming! The Swiss Are Coming!

The sharpened sticks and palm fronds make simple
the old equation: what's left to carry
after an unstoppable force meets with
an unstoppable force with meat on its breath.
I've fashioned this contraption of paddles
and rope to lift you water. There's no end
to our robot intelligence once storms
land the stern upon the shoal, and crises
learn you something of mettle and labor,
especially if the island's contents
include a team of helpful animals.
But should legality be an issue,
remember who wears the boots in a state
of nature; then walk lightly to impress
on them the realms of your beneficence—
nature will appreciate that. Still, listen
for rustlings in the bushes; you remain
a bug to them despite your best efforts
to molt. Should another captive appear
one morning, welcome her with old-style dances
and holiday totems of mud and twigs.
Don't talk about the sea, even to avoid
those awkward silences that can leave you
marooned for days. When the islanders return,
greet them with coconuts and gunpowder.

"And We Not There, Not There, Not There"

Which presupposes a theory
        of other minds,
                and that way unchecked lies
mealtime in event of aircrash
        over the Andes or
                an apocalyptic virus.
So the agon persists
        between brain and stomach
                for the seat of our good
intentions. I intend you
        this brick,
                whether you make of it
a house or hole
        through the windshield,
                I leave it to the gods,
which is to say
        ourselves, Billy Buddy, so you can see
                where ethics will lead us.
Some days, a walk in the park
        is just a walk,
                and it's the erstwhile
gentle trees that have gone
        corporate, drinking dry
                that aquifer of dollars.
Some days you come up
        standing in the sea
                at the shore, facing
inland. If it would have you,
        you'd lie down;
                if there were an escape hatch,

you'd flirt with the latch.
But the reality of you
getting on the train is
you are on the train, and
being the conductor
is probably just as miserable
and mindless as you think,
with only so many permutations
of a gapping maw
you can pretend you're entering after
innuendo goes stale;
and the flashing board—
with its worn out buttons—barely
beeps now and then;
and sometimes it's *you*
who jumps onto the tracks
to cover with *your* body
the fallen
grandmother of twenty;
sometimes there's not even
the train or people at all
there, or even the city, the planet,
the whole swirling
mess of gasses and ice
and cosmic blind spots, gone,
when you get around
to imagining it.

No IEDs

As a leaf
might wing
against the you

you're opening
to along the
road

susceptible
in the light
we enter

the islanded content of
this sudden
daisy-chain

Carlsbad Caverns, New Mexico, May 2010

Because in all great stories you must descend
                    into the deep,—and though not great, we go
          down into it, having acquired our guide,

since there's always a guide, the one who knows
                    the forest path, the cave, the requisite
          rituals and incantations, what charms,

what gifts to coax the dead, because the dead
                    have what we're after and keep the way out—
          so we're invited by Ben, our park ranger

in shorts and tucked-in shirt the desiccated
                    colors of Sybil's leaves, to touch the stone
          greased by the decades of visitors' palms,

a plan, Ben says, to conserve the living rock
                    below, the millennia of minerals
          spiked and swelling as water's residue.

And what is it that will be scoured from us
                    as the residue of fire? The detritus stuck
          between the wheels we'll be churned in and past?

And if all my unkindnesses from first to last
                    could be recalled like so much sand to mark
          the time I must pay back, then there is work

for justice to perform, to ask each crime
to reenact its suffering as its fine,
for each broken faith another skin to bear

in hand, like Michelangelo's self carried
down to judgment by St. Bartholomew.
When the elevator doors open

it's a landscape crawled up from underwater
and vaguely sexual like an Ernst painting.
I imagine the first mortal to enter

here, the country he found in his meager light.
To have our turn at the nipple-shaped stalagmite,
we check our flashes and file into the queue.

After Petrarch

I.

O scattered

over what I fed into

with error after error,

I was not the same man (this ground

is deep).

May I find mercy

after love's trials,

for all the ways in

lead through the throes,

and I have seen enough in this land:

a whole people like a tale

of my own name,

of all my harvest;

and what pleases is swift.

II.

It was swift, the pleasure of your body

felt along the length of me,

the permission a crowd gives

when pressing through a bar,

then the crush against

the scrawl on the bathroom wall,

saying what the tongue would do

and was doing, but before

in the taxi from Lincoln to Wicker Park,

something dissolved into—

what your eyes augured flickered

across the windows of mine:

your arced back lifting silver

rings into my mouth.

In the House of Aphrah

It came as a film, a light texture felt
like what a word might make spoken against
your skin, so a slight pressure you could take
away moving your hand away, or how

withdrawing my fingers from the keyboard
where—refreshed—I was given the instant
feeds, I found the word *dust*. Then someone else
saw it as grit in the eye, so not dust

itself but a watery lens that sprang
from the irritant—dunes and eclipses,
redactions and detentions we would now
meet through, and the dust accumulated.

Some discovered the dust between their teeth
like raspberry seeds, something to work with
the tongue, to jaw when speaking, and in speaking,
knew dust. But everyone was embarrassed,

unsure it wasn't only on their breath,
clotting their speech. Then a first hand caught dust
pressed on the palm it coupled, the throat it set
upon, the body brought close in the dark.

Times Being What They Are

I thought about a fish,
a glinting something
capable of rising towards
        the surface.

***

Not knowing whether
the instinct's to fight or fuck,
but that's not the saying.

***

Hard to connect that
to here, the cordage
too frayed—it's grown
        too many tendrils.

***

A slip happens like the gears
not timed to the teeth, where
the words get away with
        the mind's momentum.

***

Surge, insurgency, waves
and waves of it.
It happens everyday—

***

the cell phone dials up nails;
the breakfast will be interrupted;
the packet of gum turns out
          to be cocaine.

***

Something silver, something
I might reach down into and feel—
so I've read—the burn of
          what I learn there.

***

Forty or four, the exchange
seems simple. Just cover
the mouth, the yawn, the "O."

***

What a trash, what a time-
table for the extraction! The reports
have a crowd of nearly a hundred
around the celebrity's SUV.

***

But it despises the air,
and how it breathes can hurt you,
and the tail turns back into the glass.
You can never live there.

Epistle

And so all day I've been working over
a phrase, B_____, some articulation meant
to give shape to the feeling caught inside it,

the imprecise one, a speck stumbling around
the eye, an insect kicking its way through gel—
and sometimes what is moving so near to you,

the expanded life, is only so many
breaths from all these people shifting in pockets
of air along the platform, and the train's suck

pulling off toward the next stop, its continued
intakes and expulsions that you'd be a fool
to mistake for any kind of sympathy,

for evidence of order beyond the snap
of the electric rails where they collect
discarded fares and fast food cups, and if

the world were not completely shot with loss,
and if when we hear it, the phrase would come—
spontaneously, inevitably—a feeling

that you've always had and can't remember
not having, but I feel I've read it somewhere:
in all important ways you are alone.

Psalm

When I saw the great flash,
when the actor's face—stricken with recognition—
struck the floor, when the earth moved
like water, a wave of ash and dust
that settled back to dust,
I knew I needed it, that you required this
from me, or I from you,
a need to know that when
all our sins, all our carelessnesses,
return real as flesh
or as close to flesh as we can bear
and still have the punishment
palatable—while bursting no less
acrid on the tongue, no less
excruciating as hammer to thumb
for its being understandable,

which in the stories has always been
the service of angels or machines,
who arrive on the scene barreling forth
some ground-razing blaze
of your retribution—that we can make ready;
and sometimes the righteous are spared,
and sometimes the cheat, the faithless one,
the murderer is galvanized
with a new sense of mission,
swept up in the common urgency

to take whatever or whomever's left
at hand and carry them on shoulders,
on carts, on ships, the new tribe
setting out, and who will wander,
and who will suffer more in their wandering,
to found the new city.

Notes

"Auspices." The final two quotes come from N.W.A.'s "Appetite for Destruction" and Ice Cube's "We Had to Tear This Mothafucka Up," respectively.

"Pax Americana." The last sentence of the first stanza makes reference to Albert Camus's *Notebooks: 1935-1951*. The last sentence of the final stanza is a translation of the opening to Horace's Ode III.6.

"To the Architects of Our Present Misfortune." The movie is Alex Proyas's *Dark City*. The Italian is Dante. The attitudes toward the California wild fires are a reference to Enron energy traders as represented in Alex Gibney's documentary *Enron: The Smartest Guys in the Room*. The poem closes with an allusion to an episode in the life of Julius Caesar as reported by Suetonius.

"Epistle" ["If I thought it would help…"]. This poem quotes from *Moby Dick*, David Ferry's translation of Horace's Epistle I.6, Kenneth Burke's *A Rhetoric of Motives*, and the "A Hole in the World" episode of Joss Whedon's *Angel*. The anecdote about the man in the bar is a reference to a sketch for a story in Albert Camus's *Notebooks: 1935-1951*. This poem is dedicated to Brian Nicolet.

"Clarissa in Uptown." Clarissa is Virginia Woolf's Clarissa Dalloway.

"Fear and Trembling." Section two is from the perspective of Socrates, conflating Plato's *Apology* and *Crito* dialogues. The italicized phrases in section four come from W.H. Auden's "Musée des Beaux Arts."

"From the Provinces." Section v. The italicized portions come from a Human Rights Watch interview with Musli Hoxhaj, the sole survivor of a massacre at Golubovac, Kosovo. Thirteen men were beaten, shot, and killed in the garden. Section vi. On November 3, 1998, the people of Minnesota elected former wrestling star Jesse "The Body" Ventura as Governor of the state. The italicized portions of this section come from Roland Barthes's

"The World of Wrestling," in *Mythologies*, tr. Annette Lavers.

"Ecology." This poem owes its structure to Rick Barot's "Litany."

"In an Adirondack with You." This poem is a pastiche of Coleridge's "This Lime-Tree Bower My Prison." It is for Merrill Feitell and Matt Hart.

"Epistle" ["Because sleep won't come…"]. This poem quotes and adapts phrases from Shakespeare's *Hamlet*, Clarence Brown and W.S. Merwin's translation of Osip Mandelstam's poem "126," *The Sopranos*, John Donne's "The Funeral," *Annie Hall*, and Keats's May 10-11, 1817, letter to Benjamin Robert Haydon.

"The Pure Products." The title comes from William Carlos Williams's "To Elsie." The quoted phrases are from Williams's "The Botticellian Trees" and "Genesis."

"And We Not There, Not There, Not There." The title comes from William Carlos Williams's "The Birth of Venus."

"Times Being What They Are." The title comes from Tom Stoppard's *Rosencrantz and Guildenstern Are Dead*. The poem quotes a phrase from Sylvia Plath's "Lady Lazarus."

Acknowledgments

Grateful acknowledgment is made to the editors of the following journals in which poems from this collection have previously appeared in these and other versions:

BODY; Cerise Press; *Copper Nickel*; *The Delmarva Review*; *Forklift, Ohio; Green Mountains Review; Grist; Hotel Amerika; Literary Imagination; The Minnesota Review*; *New South*; *Southwest Review*; *Third Coast*; *The Washington Post*; and *Witness.*

I am also grateful to family, friends, and the institutions whose support and community made these poems possible, particularly Kent Shaw, Brian Nicolet, Joseph Campana, Nick Flynn, Dominic Smith, David Haynes, the Bread Loaf Writers' Conference, and the University of Houston Creative Writing Program and English Department. And I am thankful to Holly Holmes for joining me in "going across this river willy-nilly."

Paul Otremba is the author of one previous poetry collection, *The Currency* (Four Way Books, 2009). His poems, reviews, and criticism have appeared in such places as *American Poets in the 21st Century: The New Poetics, The Houston Chronicle, The Kenyon Review, Literary Imagination, New England Review, Poetry Daily, Southwest Review,* and *The Washington Post.* He lives in Houston, Texas.

Publication of this book was made possible by grants and donations. We are also grateful to those individuals who participated in our 2014 Build a Book Program. They are:

Nickie Albert
Michele Albright
Whitney Armstrong
Jan Bender-Zanoni
Juanita Brunk
Ryan George
Michelle Gillett
Elizabeth Green
Dr. Lauri Grossman
Martin Haugh
Nathaniel Hutner
Lee Jenkins
Ryan Johnson
Joy Katz
Neal Kawesch
Brett Fletcher Lauer & Gretchen Scott
David Lee
Daniel Levin
Howard Levy
Owen Lewis
Paul Lisicky
Maija Makinen
Aubrie Marrin
Malia Mason
Catherine McArthur
Nathan McClain
Michael Morse
Chessy Normile
Rebecca Okrent
Eileen Pollack
Barbara Preminger
Kevin Prufer
Soraya Shalforoosh
Alice St. Claire-Long
Megan Staffel
Marjorie & Lew Tesser
Boris Thomas
William Wenthe